SIGHTING THE SLAVE SHIP

Sighting the Slave Ship

PAULINE STAINER

BLOODAXE BOOKS

ISBN: 1 85224 176 4

First published 1992 by
Bloodaxe Books Ltd,
P.O. Box 1SN,
Newcastle upon Tyne NE99 1SN.

Bloodaxe Books Ltd acknowledges
the financial assistance of Northern Arts.

Cover reproduction by V & H Reprographics, Newcastle upon Tyne.

Cover printing by J. Thomson Colour Printers, Glasgow.

Printed in Great Britain by
Bell & Bain Limited, Glasgow, Scotland.

for John

Acknowledgements

Acknowledgements are due to the editors of the following publications in which some of these poems first appeared: *Argo, Christian Poetry 1989, Critical Survey, The Frogmore Papers, Grand Piano, The Green Book, Images, Lines Review, Manchester Poetry 2* and *4, New Spokes, Oxford Magazine, The Poetry Book Society Anthology 1988–89* (PBS/ Hutchinson, 1988), *Poetry Matters 8* (Peterloo Poets, 1990), *Prospice, The Rialto, Skoob Review, Staple,* and *The Times Literary Supplement.*

'A Haze held by Thorns' and 'The Red King's Dream' were commissioned by the Brotherhood of Ruralists and published in *The Secret Garden* (1989) and *Some Thoughts on Alice* (1990).

I should like to acknowledge a Fellowship in Creative Writing at Hawthornden Castle, where many of these poems were written.

Contents

Sighting the Slave Ship

We came to unexpected latitudes –
sighted the slave ship
during divine service
on deck.

In earlier dog-days
we had made landfall
between forests of sandalwood,
taken on salt, falcons and sulphur.

What haunted us later
was not the cool dispensing
of sacrament
in the burnished doldrums

but something more exotic –
that sense
of a slight shift of cargo
while becalmed.

Piranesi's Fever

It could have been malaria –
the ricochet of the pulse
along his outflung arm,
grappling-irons
at each cautery-point on the body.

She lay with him between bouts;
pressed to his temple
the lazy estuary of her wrist;
brought him myrrh
on a burning salver.

How lucid they made him,
the specifics against fever:
the magnified footfall of the physician,
the application of cupping-glasses
above the echoing stairwell,

windlass and shaft,
the apparatus of imaginary prisons;
a catwalk slung across the vault
for those who will never take
the drawbridge to the hanging-garden.

None of this he could tell her –
that those he glimpsed
rigging the scaffold
were not fresco-painters,
but inquisitors giddy from blood-letting;

that when he clung to her
it wasn't delirium
but a fleeting humour of the eye –
unspecified torture,
death as an exact science.

Only after each crisis, could he speak
of the sudden lit elision
as she threw back the shutters
and he felt the weight of sunlight
on her unseen breasts.

Paul Klee at Pompeii, 1902

Piranesi came before you –
sketched the footings
of the dead streets,
left you the glass-tesserae.

Lasers detect ancient sunlight,
but not how you tilted
magic squares
into impulse of grief;

and for us, caught
between polarities:
the colour-grid,
the haze over floating landscape,

that imagined plumage
before the bird alights
on the pastoral
under the ash –

whose foot sounds
above the grating,
which body falls
against the unearthed fresco

when memory perfects
as if life were a lesser art?

A Haze Held by Thorns

A jeweller's wheel cuts the constellations
above the circular garden
on the single canvas

the white doe folds her feet into tallowed alabaster;
the dancers pour their shawls
like glazes over the balustrade

beside the seven immaculate triangles of water,
the dead wear their trembler-springs
of hammered gold

the sun notches its arrow;
the pomegranate bleeds;
the virgin wears an ermine on her sleeve

the timbre of the light
a haze held by thorns,
a snakeskin still perfect over the eye.

How it burns back – the myrrh at noon –
the milk from the crushed nectaries
of her breasts –

and beyond the palings,
where the paired birds hang
on their frieze

the falconers
walk into the crucifixion.

The Blue Beret
(after Rembrandt)

In the *Raising of the Cross*
you painted yourself
in a blue beret
assisting at the crucifixion.

Is death
so fixed a tincture
none at the atrocity
escape recognition?

Soft –
even now
in the *Descent by Torchlight*
you help him down,

wearing neither beret
nor doublet,
but bodies
interlaced

for flesh
is the outlandish dress
at the recurring
deposition.

To Saskia, with Pearls in her Hair

(after Rembrandt)

Four pregnancies
and only one surviving son –
I sketched your dishevelled sheets
for the *Death of the Virgin.*

Painting your last portrait,
I remembered how I had drawn you
in silverpoint
three days after our betrothal;

how for an early etching
you wore a fillet of warm pearls,
and when I made
the first pure pull from the plate

I saw your breast
through the split bodice
whiter than
the shaft of a quill.

Villanelle for the Black Prince

These are the funeral achievements:
as they moved the helm from the tomb
the soft white moths flew out;

gauntlets lined with uterine kid
for the metacarpal bones,
these are the funeral achievements;

the gipon quartered with lambswool,
eye-slits below the fleur-de-lis –
the soft white moths flew out;

felines crouching on the knuckles
like pall-weights,
these are the funeral achievements;

a quilted beast for a crest,
lozenges stencilled inside the mouth –
the soft white moths flew out.

The achieve-of, the mastery of the thing
the leopard roaring without a tongue –
these are the funeral achievements,
the soft white moths flew out.

The Red King's Dream
(for Graham Arnold)

It is one of those white stone days;
the Reverend Charles Dodgson
is in his darkroom
developing on large glass plates
the exposures
of a girl's body.

I look through the key-hole
into the Deanery garden,
sisters on the croquet lawn,
the air full of hedgehogs
up, down, strange, charmed
like quarks

my queen scowls
at the topiary
a quickset hog shot up
into a porcupine,
a lavender pig with sage
growing in its belly

gauzes drop from the fly-tower;
the Furies are for real,
endgame an axe –
the alchemist
dressed in tinsel
hanged with a yellow rope

but time runs slower
nearer the earth;
the oars are feathered,
the executioner
pelted with roses,
and from a skep

on the White Knight's saddle,
bees swarm into
the scented rushes
where a girl holds
mirror-writing
to the river.

Song of the Master Mason

Like Cain
I struck him
below the sprung stone

chiselled his flesh,
jealous
of such apprenticeship.

I have wept
that my wellspring
should be a boy's body

my mason's mark
the dead
cut to the quick

the dark currency
of miracle
a tree axed at source –

those eight dragons
would suck the glancing blood
from its girth

were it not
that when I touch it
the pillar flows with his dream.

Angel-roof

They rise on bleached wings
from the pure maths
of the hammerbeams;
more frugal than El Greco's angels
who drop one wing
as if grace were mettlesome.

What startles
is not how they blanch the dusk;
but the tilted roof-mirror
which magnifies their wounds
for their breasts
are peppered with shot;

and outside, untouched by such candour,
disparate fuses burn;
sheep graze the salt-marsh,
and brushing the transepts,
the faint rank hawthorn
races the blood.

Jacob and the Angel

(after Epstein)

It is sexual –
their wrestling
on the bright pavement

bodies fiercely touching
at loin, not lip,
an alabaster blaze in the blood

the man yielding
to driven-light
in the seed

then stillness,
momentary, monumental –
as of doves mating.

Structuring the Silence

This is the landscape
of the Old Masters:
the single figure fishing
below the precipice,
the floating sleeve
of the mist.

Our horses hesitate
before the steel hawser
across the bridleway,
the pungency
of riffled sawdust,
the felled tree.

We date the core
in the failing light;
see where the outer rings
flow together as if
to assimilate the sun,
gaze at the stain of impact;

remember the red-earth
calligraphy
freely painted
under the glaze
of the Chinese pillow
for the dead

and having abstracted
the oracle-bones from silence,
felled stillness
at a stroke –
we sway slightly
like spirits balancing in the saddle

and ride on.

Transparencies in a Landscape

Speedskaters *en grisaille*
streaking the fen
like trace over smoked paper

a heron on the ice,
fish suspended
into steel-engraving

deer grazing
the moon from the leaves:
the moment at gaze.

Time is dense with such inclusions –
vesicles in the rock,
crystals that grow in the body

the luminous inconsequence of
the sign which suffices;
adze and ripple

of riverlight
through the split
where the arrow is notched

our lips wet
with the brief dew that falls
during eclipse.

Zen and the Amazon Moonflower

It opens within an hour
inconsequent
as all night-flowers
that close
when light returns

but to time that ripple –
the moment
of hushed divesting,
the heavy perfume
windlessly dispersed

is to disclose
the sharp cry of the samurai
who bears the death-poem
bound to his quiver
like a bloom

Fanfare for Recovered Sounds

In the salt-mines
the jazz trumpeters
shake out their spittle,
locate the echo

Tutankhamun's trumpet
last blown
at the ceremony
for the opening of the mouth

mute flourish
of mouthpiece and valve
the subtle body,
the *pneuma* at Ypres

Miles Davis
double-tonguing
the single note
with which, as a boy

he saw gas-burners
catch alight.

An Improvisation for Satie

After your death
they found in your room
a large number of identical grey suits,
curious sketches in the cigar-box
of meres at the time of Charlemagne;

slight harmonic shifts
for indifferent light,
birds as vapours
on the edge of an alembic,
rising-mist in the heronry;

no lake
translucent enough
for glazing the fen,
the dissonance
from the glistening peat –

slip-knot
and open-work bonnet,
the sublimation
of hazel-rods
impaling the body;

the estuary beyond
wearing moving-flaws
in the glass;
then sudden ebb –
a silent widening

of the wake –
the sureness with which
to equivocate,
light snow falling
light snow falling.

Music for Invasive Surgery

Hush is unnecessary.
Surgeons operate on the ear
to the sound of string quartets.

Hands make division on a ground:
moving parts are revealed
like a skeleton clock.

Why is excision
the most haunting
of disciplines –

the divining of affliction
never appropriate –
the music to which the unicorn kneels

death and the maiden?

Underglaze Blue

This is the underglaze blue:
the orchestra
glimpsed at dusk
through issuing-vapours
from the cloister;

suppliant strings –
the rising-damp
in the piazza
stealing the rosin
from our bows.

We remembered the Jewish quartet
putting on their bone-mutes,
other musicians
coming through the mist
bearing instruments of peace.

Our torches blew out in the wind
but we played on
for the Immortals
giving audience
in a continuous landscape.

The Occluder

She is not anaesthetised
but listens to Mozart
while the cardiologists
lodge a tiny blocking-device
in the holes of her heart

the guide wire
fed through an artery
from groin to aorta,
a catheter inserted,
the blood slaked by occlusion;

but o strange haemorrhage –
the red tracer
in the one flesh –
the Mozart lovers
running the concentration camps

the inmate
who every day
sketched the mounting pile
of bodies
against the wire

so absorbed by their pallors
under snowfall
it became a technique
to prevent bleeding
through the heartwall.

The Ringing Chamber

I was four months gone –
my breasts already tender
against the bell-ropes;

we were ringing quarter-peals,
the sun flooding the bell-chamber,
the dust rippling between the joists

when the child quickened,
fluttered against the changes;
and suddenly through the clerestory

I saw that colder quickening –
random, reciprocal –
cloudshadow

and the flaxfield
like water under the wind.

Skydivers

They fall outwards
as if from the calyx of a flower
each smaller than a falcon's claw,
their target a gravel circle
in the Byzantine barley.

They fall like hushed flame
where once the sun's disk
was ploughed from the furrow,
coupling, uncoupling
above the drop-zone.

When they run
with the white squall
you would think the air
holds their flight
like a welder's seam,

but as they alight
there's a sudden
billow of pollen,
an uprush
from winged heels

and like lovers,
the sweet tarrying
of their bodies
dissolves
the moment.

The Falconer's Bride

Before the hawking party
you stroked the falcon's breast
with a little switch;

showed me the immature plumage,
transparent hunger-traces on the welts,
the shafts still full of blood.

It was a skill you said
to keep a hawk from sleeping,
marry its speed with the wind.

I have embroidered lure and hood with noble metals;
cut from supple leather
the sliding-jesses worn even in flight.

You gave me the white gyrfalcon in Lent;
but today, I remembered
how you filled your mouth with water,

sprayed it through closed lips
onto the restive bird's breast –
and her sudden pure mantling.

The Hawking Party

They walked out from the wood
at the edge
of the old airfield,
clad in brown and green,
the girl with a stripped hazel wand
in her hand

their hawks barefaced
but they oblique,
for they neither looked up nor spoke,
passing in profile
as from the fresco
of an Italian master

and since,
I have heard the stoop
whistle like a bullet
and the first snow sift the iron leaves
more faintly than the shift of talons
along a gloved fist

as if the accessories of falconry
were not perishable.

The Yew Walk

What is the distance
between us, you said
when we slept naked
but barely touched;
the quilt thrown back,
streaks of moth-dust
across your breast.

That night I dreamt
you brushed against
the trees of the yew-walk;
the strange fine pollen dust
shook out,
sifted most eerily
inside your dress.

I do not know
why its green-gold
so long unloosed
kindled your nakedness –
or why I woke to kiss
the estranging dust
the single flesh.

The Victorian Head Dress

I dreamt I had to find it
for my second wedding,
with its seed-pearls
and lilies
on their silvered wire.

The whole light summer night
I searched;
wondered why we furnish the dead
when the living wear
such stiff flowers.

The wedding-car came,
the solstice whitened
over the salt-marsh,
refracted wading-birds
knelt in the silt

but how coldly it flared —
the wax in my hair;
and through the windscreen
the glass-cage
of the sun.

The Reprieve

If I did not see them at first
it was because
they were skating on sunlight,
the shin-bones of animals
shaped to fit
under their shoes.

I never knew
whether it was pollen in the wind
or refracted sun from the saltings
which gave them
the cunning tooling
of haloes.

You said later
you had missed them;
but I saw you
among the cloud of witnesses –
unaccountably silenced
by the kiss of their blades.

Leonardo draws Bernardo Bandini

(hanged for the murder of Giuliano de Medici)

You noted the costume
as if compiling an inventory:
tan-coloured cap,
doublet of black serge,
dark hose;
red-stippled velvet
at the swinging neck.

How cool a faculty,
when you bequeathed
no silver instruments of surgery,
but drew
soft against stopped heart,
a blue coat lined
with fur of foxes' breasts.

A Party of Musicians in a Boat

No inventory mentions them –
though precious pigments
are noted:
two florins for ultramarine.

What is their pedigree –
those who beguiled
the Madonna of the Little Masters
with divisions on a ground?

Little is needed
to improvise against melancholy:
hour-glass and dividers,
a composition of figures.

Did they play for Leonardo
who strung the silver-skull,
when lakes were shoaled
with hibernating swallows?

Mysterious are those
painted to music;
but what of these
raising the burnished spinnaker?

Will the wind take their sails?
Even at the Annunciation
the sand runs
through the hour-glass.

How is it
they withhold
so hauntingly
the timing of departure –

shrouds
bright against the light,
the blood-red drummer
beating the silent bar?

Watteau's Crucifixion

Master of ambiguity –
what lovely conspiracy
did you make of crucifixion
in a southern landscape?

Was the cross snakewood,
angels rippling
against alluvial gold
like a new shift of sails?

Is that Gilles
sanguine under eclipse
who cannot lift the body
for weight of myrrh?

Do the mourning women
wear slipper-satin
of a yellow
that physics sparrowhawks?

Did you take
straight vermilion
for the electuary
of wounds?

Do you know whether
the pilgrimage is over
or why the Magdalen
embarks in fugitive red?

Did you sanction her
to crouch below
the male half-nude
and weeping

slip her hand
between his legs?

Crucifixion in a Red Quarry

Not a film still –
the body held to its red fault
with balance-weights of quicksilver,

the sandstone drift
grained with footless birds
that have dropped from the transom.

Easy to raise the cross
against lodes hammered
and worked whilst hot

where reindeer and elk
share welded bone
with the arctic lemming.

Death has mettled
the silence,
veined the bloodstone;

but looking up,
you see the cold fauna
on the bright overhang

and for a moment
above the birdless cliff
the clay greening.

White Saxifrage

In the sterile ward
no flowers are allowed
for fear of infection;
but cut behind the curvature of the lens –
beyond the Pietà
an angel in saffron
appears to be gardening.

Revelation
is an angle of the light,
bees drinking
beside the marvellous event,
the wedding-supper
lit from an unseen source,
saints at dessert.

We are leavened –
poured out like lost-wax
before the unknown young man
among roses
whose light field armour
has crucifixion
etched on the breast.

But someone scares the birds
with a flare-gun;
the children with branches
in their hands
will not break off their game
for the entry
to Jerusalem.

No hour sounds
above the arcade
for the weeping disciples
except time's unreason –
absence of doves –
white saxifrage
on the way to execution.

Landscape with Arching Leopard

This is autumn's jade cup –
the felines flow over the rim;
in the glow off
the marsh at night,
one cooling tower
leans its shade on another.

Cattle graze
under the apse of the cathedral,
their flanks glistening
with cultured grafts
of gold-beater's skin;

the plough turns up
a centurion;
falcons above a field-hospital
attend the livid distance
to a winter christening.

On the far hill
a horse is struck by lightning –
the girl upon its back untouched,
except where round her neck
a crucifix has left
its pokerwork of grace.

Enclosed Wheatfield with Rising Sun

(this painting by Van Gogh once belonged to Robert Oppenheimer)

It is high summer.
I see the wheatfield
from the cell of my asylum;
when the wind blows from the south-east
I remember how the Romans
boiled saffron in the amphitheatre at Arles
to counteract the reek of blood.

I slept there in the yellow house
under a blood-red quilt;
the colours hissed
like metal in a mould;
I even flayed a frog,
held it to the great light of the Midi
for the intravenous lilt of the blood.

Some would have painted the sun
purple-black as a plum,
a fireball in the mouth
of a corpse;
or like Pentecostal flame,
dragonsblood,
one glaze bleeding into another.

I whipped it
until it cartwheeled like a sunflower
red on yellow
splashing the wheatfield
scarlet, pale sulphur,
a falcon
with a flail over its shoulder.

But last night I dreamt
of irradiating
all the colours at once –
as if the sun climbed
both sides of the canvas –
and in the silence
before the blaze

the high white note
of birds igniting
in mid-air.

Calvary after Rain

There is no spell
for vibrancy in a glass –
only quickthorn after rain
hung with notes
from a bird's throat;

the tree's sprung artery
half in bloom
half aflame –
Christ with one wrist
red over green

the other burning, burning.

Watersnake

How blackly
he wore the water,
rearing his saffron head
above the brackish cistern.

We had walked up
from the ruinous amphitheatre,
the olives birdless
in the salt wind;

it defined their shiver –
the way his liquid amber
left virtually no wake
in the sun –

but like Tiresias
before the divining draught,
he held silence
in his mouth

and it gushed again –
the oracle in the bloodstream,
the dead articulate
without their wits.

Source

Stone-masons from the monastery
work deeper and deeper
in the quarry,
always striking water
from the stone.

Meltwater roars
in the throat of the pumps,
the subsoil black
as with artesian
bleeding.

When the water runs clear
over the red rock
you hardly know
which fount
they tap

for the glancing play
between rule and source:
pure flux –
the reciprocating-pump
of the heart –

and when the sun
quickens the wellspring
that seminal bound –
the spilt-blue
of the virgin.

Metaphysical Interior
(with Tree and Waterfall)

In the smoke of the waterfall,
the philosophers kill with cast-shadow –
the ghost doubling as the player-king;

they dispute Rembrandt's inventory:
the archer's thumb-ring,
the quiver above the grave.

But make fast the running-rope –
a recent landslip has opened
one of the hanging thickets,

a watch says five minutes to midnight,
round the corner someone falls
between train and curved platform.

What is an issue of blood
when a tree springs
from the mouth

and between the leaves
siskins ignite their breasts
at the low winter sunlight –

those fleet successive glazes
before the jade cicada
is placed on the tongue of the dead?

The Dressing Station

(after Stanley Spencer)

How questionable it is –
the war artist's yellow filter –
the wounded on their mule-drawn stretchers
glowing like tallow,
the controlled bleeding of enchantment;

no battle-pavilion
rare ointment or fine linen,
but casualties aligned
in sulphurous light
between blood-red pillows;

in the makeshift theatre
a bowl of water on a tripod;
at the lit vanishing-point
alchemical figures
to draw the sheet over the face;

the black beast
of the Apocalypse
stumbling between the shafts;
a white sling
worn as triangle for redemption.

Christ to Charon

You probed my palms
with a boat-hook
as if they were runes
from a border-country.

'You a mercenary then?'
you asked
as we grounded
mid-stream.

You began
to navigate by echo:
wondered what depth of wound
you had plumbed.

But leaning
over the gunwale
you saw the rising dead
in the blood-wake

'Must mercy
be seen to bleed?'
'Compassion kills'
I said.

Goslar Warrior

(after Henry Moore)

The Greeks too are calm:
a man hurling a discus
will be caught
at the moment in which
he gathers his strength

Not for you –
you have caught
him off balance,
the tilt of the shield
against the falling warrior;

on the spinning battlefield
the ancestors
are unslaked,
their impetus
iron in the artery;

and you, the sculptor –
why should you feel
that weight in the heartwall
to control the reel
from the blade

when for a moment
the air is gifted
most terribly
with his blood
pumping?

Unearthing the Terracotta Army

You cannot prise open
their mouths
for the password –
the terracotta warriors
rated so highly in the clay
so little in the flesh;
serried
in their splashed glaze
as through a multiplying glass;

easy to disinter bone
heat-cracked
for the oracle;
to topple the head
where the knife
shaped allegiance;
their eyes open,
unlike live soldiers
who sleep at the sepulchre

but what are bodyguards –
quick veins
in a quick vault –
when centuries later
they sense
the red blood
that flows from the
artillery man's ears

and give no sign?

In a Chinese Pavilion

At the half-hour
the dragon spits a pearl
into the lotus

the mechanism of the water-clock
cut from jade so thin
it transmits the light.

The lovers walk in
from the cool dazzle
of white cherry.

Time is water weighed –
the vessels rise up
on their floats

lion and phoenix dance
and the golden ball
drops into the brazen cup.

The Airbrush Painting

She swings lightly
in her hammock
as if demineralised

the leopard-lilies
lie abroad
in their shade

she dreams
the heart is too small
for its blood

not knowing
how the god
bewilders the girl

opening her thighs
as if time
were ductile.

Fire-bringers

the air darkens
with winter swallows
in the red-light district
of Bangkok

as they drop to roost
the tattooist needles
a vivid bird
just over the breast

O sister swallow
hectic
between magnetic fields –
such flicker

and below
streetwise girls,
lovers tonguing
the vulva

Tigers Drinking

Not recent —
their hanging forms
over water —
the thin inlays
of amber and bronze

the gravels hold no print
where they slaked themselves
with translucent darks,
the river sulphurous
under a Grail moon.

Impalpable
the blooding of memory —
the disappearing yellows,
the nonchalance
of their lapping among the lilies —

even now
none know with what
burning inconsequence
their rough tongues
still kindle the ripple.

Togare

I have trained tigers
to spring at deflected light
from a dagger.

Take us on long exposure –
man and beast
ribboned with topaz like duellists.

They flinch at a flash,
brindled under the arc-lamps,
paws quilting the sawdust;

no inadvertent wound
except the sprung-release
of children

following me from the ringside
with the perishable inlay
of their eyes.

If suspended on a thread
and struck
that blade would sound

indefinitely

Mrs John Dowland

Do they ask after me
the foreign musicians,
when you play the galliard
for two upon one lute?

Cantus high on the fingerboard,
Bassus on the lower frets;
hands changing position
above the rose?

Here there is no perfect measure
for the visitation of the plague –
no resolution
for figures on a ground –

only the memory of how
you brooded over my body;
and the speaking harmony
with which, beyond all music

I would stop your lips.

The Lady's Walk

From the garden room
above the gorge
you can see the lady's walk;
fallow bucks in velvet
take the red fault through the rock.

It is the hot season,
cool only in the columbarium
and where the hawk stoops
to quick veins
in the keep.

Lady at the virginals –
no windlass
will raise or lower the angels;
the squirrel scolds,
the lovers scull below the well.

We must take the back stair:
it is the nightingale who cries
Root out the tongue
and people with questions
are arriving by boat.

Glass-men

Tonight
beyond the glow of charcoal
the gondolas leave
bluish-opal trails,
the sea-mist spiced with woodsmoke,
grids of chestnuts roasting

when the boy beckons
between the braziers
I remember the bodies
of glass-blowers, half-naked
against the furnace –
hot gathers of glass at the end
of each iron

how when they put
their salt mouths
to the blowing-rods
molten, manipulative,
I felt the lagoon rise
in the tidal dungeons.

St Sebastian

His body is juiced sweeter
than any girl's,
his tormentors
snooded in the wind.

It tilts at silence –
the way quicks
of whitethorn
lodge in his vitals

the technique of martyrdom
shafting, sexual,
a cicatrice
misterioso

How should we read
such carnal knowledge
as the wounds
whistle by?

Fabula

(after El Greco)

Why did it disturb so —

the boy lighting a candle
from a glowing coal,
the monkey looking on?

No chafing-dish or cautery-iron;
no blood drawn by vacuum
into a heated cup.

Men are instinct with light —
see how the rainbow pauses
over border-country —

yet we warmed
to that blown image
the original dusk of their being

the leering figure
of the watching youth,
wisdom kindled on a monkey's face.

Woman Holding a Balance
(after Vermeer)

We x-ray the embryo;
tap the womb
for the sex of the unborn;
but are haunted
by your composure.

Inclining your cool head,
you weigh
what we have found
questionable:
woman as diviner.

It could be gold-dust
in the scale-pans;
graded pearls;
or freight of souls
for the Last Judgement.

But the balance is empty;
and you keep
the equipoise
of anonymity
with downcast lids.

We cannot weigh
the serenity of genes;
measure purity by mirrors;
but when you
suspend the scales

You embody
such stillness,
we could believe
light from your high window
incarnates a child.

One-way Mirror

*The heart — have you found the heart?' And realising at
once that none of them had found it, they continued their
way along the corridor, tapping and listening to the mirrors.*
JEAN GENET: 'The Miracle of the Rose'

Therapy they call it —
we sit in the room with mirrors
and my daughter decides
which of her two selves
she will put on.

Even in the teaching hospital
mirrors have rites:
the healers hide behind silver,
the Magdalen, with hair unloosed,
holds candle and skull up to the glass.

I ask why the witnesses
do not sit in the same room;
the video records,
the lights flicker;
they confer invisibly.

Truth is irremediable.
Acid can shape an image on glass;
in early X-rays the photographer
guided the catheter
into his own heart.

How cool it is,
the remote control
of respective mercies,
to heal by making
the correct wound.

Madonna misericordia —
there is no mirror
for the eye of the heart;
cup your ear to the wall
*it was the executioner
who first heard the beats*

and through the glass
we bleed, we bleed.

The Water Glass

As children,
We dipped the surplus summer eggs
In waterglass for wintering;

Layered them pointed-end down,
Lightly tiered
In the cold of the slippery jar.

We would reach down to our armpits,
Through a shivered kingdom
Of refracted shells.

Above the magnified ivory,
Our faces floated on the ruffled surface,
Plumped-out or skeletal,

Apparitions of tension –
The ritual of unreal children
In a dangerous glass.

Design for a Light Machine

These are absolute measurements:
the sky precision-tooled;
no threshold of escape
until the tumbler dressed as a demon
comes up out of the trap;

all resonance the golden mean –
though those in the dry valley
still cup their ears
for voices
from behind the waterfall.

The light wits of acrobats
scissor the air;
physicists bombard gold foil
with elastic particles;
against the stars

the target-head
has a hole for trepanning;
Einstein plays Mozart
on the violin –
nothing has its proper shadow

until one summer night
an owl strikes the windscreen,
leaves in powdered impact
on the glass,
the gaze of the god revealed.

Untitled Diptych

I

Wild-fowlers
on the frozen fen
draw sledges with bone-runners
across the glittering reach
no light can date.

Such traffic on the ice –
the skaters turn their backs
as the body of a child
is handed onto the platform
before Treblinka.

II

With a glass rod
the painter has made a hole
in the ventricle of memory;
magicians convene again
in the Winter Gardens

their illusory apparatus
a dry-ice machine:
rime pricks the thatch,
emissaries bring salt, silver and amber,
the midwife bears the burial spice.

Speedskaters

They streak down
the water-grid
sexless between
the swelling sallows

bent forward
without feature
as if they have
jettisoned caprice

muscle and blade
in bloodless rhythm,
only deadline
seaming the silver.

But as they graze
the hazels,
the sudden
soft-focus lens −

pollen flurried
above the red stigma −
the steeled timing,
the rare confusion.

Stag

What was the metalled edge
along which I drove
when he sprang
from dark to dark

his head
escutcheoned
against the spinney
in the undipped lights?

Not black-ice,
the wheels locked
in skid –
but an older elision –

skeletons in
foetal position,
one of a child
cradling antlers.

.

Pentimenti

To reveal
the altered underpainting
is to take
purposeful tracks
beneath snow;

read crouched burial
into red-chalk underdrawing,
correct the incline
as grave-ships
rake the slipway.

Such revision
the singularity
by which the spirit
flexes
into Gethsemane –

the penitents
beneath the overpainted miracle
frozen into their zone
like animals
at the salt-lick

the gazelles running
in the further walled gardens
where the naked were whipped
through the iron air
till they wailed like dogs.

We perfect
by heightening the angle
at which the angel offers the cup –
as if the heart were unswerving,
the anvil alterable.

Skiing across the Ice Cap

We take the uncharted snow
under light, contrary winds;
wear visors
against the electric-blue,
move so keenly
we might be shod with bone;

each foray
tinged like first light
with every possibility:
coral at the ice cap,
pollen-grains hazing the pole,
honeycomb among ammonites.

The world shelves
to no edge;
as fresco-painters
we lay our tints
with molten speed
on the unmelting field.

Who would sweep the tracks
before sealing the tomb?
Perfect crystals occur;
a plane banks suddenly
beyond the remembered overhang
of the ice –

the serious mastery
of unfamiliar terrain
to see at proper distance
the mute lesson,
the giant talon,
the immaculate desertion.

The Release

It was white-out, they said.
They had been flying
in close formation
when he took a tangent
across the salt lake.

It reminded him
of flying over glasshouses,
salt snaking like spindrift,
the sun brazen with buzzards
through the perspex hood;

but there was no birdstrike —
neither blood nor feathers —
only his seat-harness released,
the parachute
shredded on the cockpit.

Later, the salvage-party lounged
under liquid amber trees,
the smoke from their fire
drifting across the fuselage
as they drowsed

between the blinding lake
and the dropping oils,
never asking whether his oxygen-mask
was disconnected before
or after.

Equipping the Spirit

They have made a hole
below the pyramid
with a carbide-tipped drill,
lowered the camera
onto libation tables
of blue granite.

It startles –
the physicality of afterlife –
the dead pulling flax
with gilded nails,
seven celestial cows
reclining

the sacred eye
restored to its socket,
each mummy flanked
by vertical snakes
with oblong hearts,
the sons of Horus
levitating above the lotus;

but is the heart weighed
with or without blood?
For in the nesting coffins
the sky-goddess
straddles the king
and the sun roars
between the lions of the horizon.

An Abstract for Leda and the Swan

'showing not so much objects as my excitement about them'
MOHOLY-NAGY

What are those limbs, magician?
a girl and a bird
burning breast to breast.

Spirals embrace –
the blood sublimes
like ice.

Which substance will
condense their snow?
Which plastics

ghost
their disembodiment
in space

the urgent axis
as his feathers oil
her nakedness?

Cocteau and the Equilibrist

He watches me, even at rehearsals,
brooding over
the imagined applause,
the glisten of sweat
on the nape of my neck.

I am Barbette
transvestite rope-walker,
my soles sensitive
as those of Chinese Women
wading naked for jade.

I wear weightless silk
of a blue that lightens
at dusk,
dance to multiple shadows
as if accompanied.

How casual I make it seem –
the controlled tremor
between movements,
the act
timed to perfection.

I never meet his gaze;
but after the last glissade
when I push past him
the rope burns again
between my thighs.

Hardy supervises the removal of graves
for a railway cutting

Even as apprentice,
the unswerving vision –
coffins along the iron road,
flare-lamps
whitening at dawn
under St Pancras,
and to the lit edge
of each bright pit,
their pelts irradiate with drizzle,
lowland foxes, lightly running.

Brunel Springs the Bridge

They drew me across
as I was dying.
I lay on my back,
heard the rumble of the open wagon,
watched the girders thresh overhead.

How busy the air was
at this altitude;
burnished insects
dropped past me
mating;

the stress
above the estuary
not pier and cantilever,
but gossamer
snagged on my waistcoat,

those random things
which had burned
there always,
invisible
as noon-tapers.

Modern Angels
Eight poems after Eric Ravilious

*In 1942, Eric Ravilious was sent as a war-artist
to Iceland. On September 2nd, the aircraft in which
he was a passenger, failed to return.*

1. *The Exercise*

You glimpsed it once –
the perfect hieroglyph
of a young pilot plunging
on training session into the dark sea
when *the exercise had to go on.*

Always you'd painted bright displacement:
the unquiet radiance of empty rooms,
a brazen ship's screw
on a wagon in snowscape,
the odd angle of those sleeping in the fuselage.

Lastly, sketchbook in hand,
you left on a patrol from Iceland,
never knowing how that exercise too –
the war-artist on active service –
ruthless, shining, would go on.

2. *Spitfires on a Bright Runway*

They stand in their rippled reflection
exact
but for mysterious digits;

their sprung-release
held glistening under watercolour –
as if the painter knew

beyond, on the ancient fen,
a breached dyke
has flooded the deer-park
and the deer wade
into the swollen waters
jostling, glittering

against the sun.

3. *Sussex Quarry at Night*

Here, where the chalk figures
flow with the downs,
you watched engines whiten
under arc-light and flare
with fine powder from the quarry;

men as magicians
at the exposed chalk wall,
exotic particles
settling in the hot slipstream
as in a winter garden;

each step a white flaw underfoot;
hedges shrouded
as if to deaden vibration;
no stranger palimpsest
till later

from the train window
you saw the body of the wheat
lean with the wind,
and turf-cutters scour
the white horse beyond

to purest bone.

4. *Hares Manoeuvring*

*'And the following day we asked the whole searchlight
party in to eat large hares...'* ERIC RAVILIOUS

In peacetime
we would catch them in our undipped lights
on the old airfield,
their spoor swerving down the frosted runway,
their gaze red.

Hypnotic
such searchlight on the retina –
each skull whittled
by darkness
to the blazing nerve;

a riving Cowper knew,
opening his little hatch
in the still square at Olney
to watch the hares gambol
against the heightening dusk

their eyes rubied,
their grey necessity
to out-manoeuvre madness –
for only after deliberate play
did the quiet quicken.

5. *Magnetic Minefield*

You had always
used light coolly
as if moving glass gaming-pieces;

found the most dangerous work
at low-tide
salving mines from the oyster-beds;

so it came luminously,
the posting to Iceland –
ivory seascape in relief

danger made pure.

6. *De-icing aircraft under the midnight sun*

This is the blue hour
which pigment and palette
will kindle and dispossess;

pillars of red light
to stimulate the heart;
the swung-lamp of the sun

illumining water-worn ammonites
in the glacier,
bluish, luminous,

and beyond,
more terrible than ice,
radials blading the wingspan

propellors of spun-blood.

7. *The Sealskin Gloves*

It was your first
and only letter from Iceland;
you asked if I would like
a pair of sealskin gloves –
What size shall I buy, you said.

None of the wariness
of a last self-portrait,
face almost erased –
Draw round your hand you said
a week after your death.

8. *Modern Angels*

We glimpse it still –
the spatial mystery of the machine –
a broken water-turbine
in a stream;
wrecked harriers
beached like modern angels
on strange shores;

pleasure-steamers
ghosting the night
in their winter quarters;
the speaking-tubes
on the bridge of the destroyer
springing like African lily
under shelling at sea;

infernal engines
on a bright slipway –
and from the flightdeck,
with all the inconsequence
of revelation,
the crossing arcs
of afterburn.